The Christ Within Revealed

C. C. Askings

Other Books by C. C. Askings:

The Christ Within Revealed, Book 1

The Christ Within Revealed, Book 2

This book is channeled material and all rights are reserved and no part of the publication may be reproduced, distributed, or transmitted in any form or by any means, or stored in a database or retrieval system, without the express and prior written consent of the publisher.

Printed in the United State of America

All Right Reserved

Copyright December, 2011

ISBN-13: 978-1468130010

ISBN-10: 1468130013

Channeling the Spirit of Christ

Book 3

C. C. Askings

Indie Author

Forward

I have to admit that when the author, C.C. Askings, approached me about the publication of this series of books, I was skeptical. I thought it was very presumptuous to assume that this particular entity or spirit could be channeled.

After reading the work, my mind and heart were changed on this matter. I could see and feel the complete and utter spirit of love offered from the personal Christ that is within each of us as each of these books reveal. What better time than now for Christ to give his true and real message to the world? A message that is down-to-earth and easily understood by children and adults alike.

Some channeled material seems difficult to understand, but the message of each volume in Books 1, 2, and 3 is clear and simple. It is written for the common man and woman, for the masses, from The Christ who walked through life as a carpenter, a fisherman, a brother, a son, a friend and a teacher. As such, this book is presented in its original inspired condition as dictated to the author and without any editing or changes by the publisher.

I can only hope that you will read this life-changing material with an open mind and heart so that you may also receive its true message of love.

Love and light,

Chariss K Walker

Question 1

Here we are again, working on Book 3 in the series of channeled messages. It is the end of 2011 and soon the beginning of 2012. Many are fearful of what will happen in 2012 at the end of the Mayan calendar. What would you say to those who believe it is the end of time?

2012 is a time of great mystery for there are many opposing beliefs about its importance. Some believe it is the end of this world as you know it while others believe it is the beginning of a new era for this world. Some believe it is a shaking away much like an earthquake while others believe it to be a birthing process.

Do not be afraid. Hold fast to your gifts during this period of transition. Be prepared. You have been given many teaching instructions in these works and in so many others. If you have worked with these methods you have nothing to fear. And if you have not worked with the instructions that have been given to you specifically, work with them now.

You would not step into the cockpit of an airplane and hope that you could fly it without taking hours of instruction. Nor should you hope to weather the flight ahead without hours of instruction.

Be prepared.

Question 2

How do we prepare for 2012?

The Universe has sent a multitude of information to you to assist in your prepare. There have been many books written to instruct you. You must open the heart to these messages and empty the mind of the history and doctrines you have been taught. Many of you have accepted the teaching of your fathers and grandfathers without allowing the heart to lead you into truth.

It is time to let go of these old views. It is time to awaken to all the information that is being sent your way by Divine providence. Do you not know that the Universe conspires on your behalf?

Do you not know that your Father/Mother will not abandon you?

Open your heart to the wisdom and understanding that flows to you from many sources, all prepared for you by Universal providence.

Read and study all that you can. Open yourselves to the understanding that is now available to you. The energetic fields and patterns of Earth are conducive to your acceptance of love and oneness. Now, more than ever before!

The information is all around you but you must open to it; you must reach out and take your gifts.

Question 3

How do we reach out and take our gifts?

Your gifts are wrapped in pretty boxes, sitting at your front door. Bring the boxes inside, unwrap the gifts, take them out of the boxes and use them. Play with them, get to know them, and treasure them.

If the gift you have received is unfamiliar to you, research and study it. Learn of its value and appreciate the gift. Accept the gift and utilize it.

These are simple instructions and although metaphorical in a sense also literal. These instructions, if followed, will open your understanding of these gifts so that you might reach out and take them as your own.

Question 4

How can the instruction be both metaphorical and literal?

My description of your gifts in the pretty boxes is metaphorical because you must use the heart to see the gifts that are waiting for you. But in order to utilize the gifts you must literally work with the gifts and get to know them intricately. If you do not understand the gift, then you must research it so that you can know all there is about how to best utilize your particular gift(s).

Do not be afraid.

Do not allow others to hinder you or dissuade you about your gift.

Do not allow others to take away the power of your gift by their lack of understanding.

Take your gift and hold fast to it.

Question 5

What are some of the gifts that are waiting for us?

There are many gifts during this time of transition.

Empathy, clairvoyance, clairaudient, channeling, healing, seers, readers, visions, dreams, dream interpretation, intuition, remote viewing, materialization, energy and time manipulation, crossing-over departed spirits, light bearers and shape shifting, are just a few.

Question 6

All I can say is "Wow!" Some of these, well actually most of these gifts have been criticized by the church for centuries. How do Christians overcome the taboo and "sin" associated with these in order to accept and receive them as gifts?

Throughout history mankind has had access to these gifts. Even in the churches there have been wise ones, those who spoke with tongues, those who had the gift of sight or healing.

It has been the leaders and rulers who forbade the use of these spiritual gifts from fear or jealousy of those who possessed them. It is those who control and rule over you that forbid the use of your gifts. It is the old guard that desires your enslavement and it is the old guard that must be thrown down and cast off.

Accept your gifts now and use them.

Do not be afraid of those who would condemn you.

Are these not gifts of the spirit? Are these not gifts from your Father/Mother?

What God has given to you, let no man take from you.

Question 7

Why have rulers and leaders forbidden the use of these gifts?

Only those who have moved into the fourth dimension or beyond have access to these gifts. Rulers and leaders are for the most part living in the third dimension, that dimension of power and control. They do not value love over fear. They have not yet moved into the realm of love which conquers all; they still believe that "might through war" conquers all.

With this type of leadership, you are nothing more than slaves. You are inferior to their way of thinking and it is unheard of that someone inferior would have a gift or power that they do not have.

Therefore, if you have such a power you must be seen as unreliable at best or of the devil at worst.

This is the old guard – alive in the ego. The old guard must be cast off by mankind in order to bring in the new reign of the heart and is ruled by love.

Question 8

Many of these gifts are associated with witchcraft and that seems to be the reason given for banning their use. How do we know we won't be accused of witchcraft for using these gifts?

You cannot receive these gifts and the ability to use them if you are not living in the heart. The heart is light and love. Nothing associated with darkness can live in the light. Light prevails over all things. Love prevails over all things.

Do not be afraid of these old superstitions. Your gifts come from the heart and it is from the heart that you will use them.

Question 9

I have known men and women who possessed such gifts and they are considered outcasts of society. Many have been medicated and called insane; some have been institutionalized. Some use their gifts to harm or control others. There is a great fear of being different in our world. How can we reconcile using these gifts when most consider them a curse rather than a gift?

The gifts of the heart are a blessing of love. Love can never be a curse. Do not be afraid of the gifts of love.

There has always been both dark and light. Those who use their gifts to harm others are products of society. They have been ridiculed for so long and talked to in such a negative manner that they have become negative.

The old guard would have you afraid to use your gifts. It is another form of enslavement. When you are beaten down by your masters, it is difficult to see the light.

After the great shift, only those living in the heart will have the ability to use these gifts. The gifts I speak of come from the Source of All Light.

Why would you be afraid of the very Source from whence you descended?

I say again, accept these gifts and become familiar with them. Be prepared for the time will come when your gifts will help others to find the light.

Question 10

I have read about the Indigo children… It is said that they have incarnated during this time remembering why they are here. What can you tell us about these children?

It is true that the Indigo child remembers his/her purpose. They have been sent to help overthrow the old guard. They are teachers to those who have been enslaved by the old guard thinking and way of life.

You will know them by their authority and purpose.

Look into the face of an Indigo child and you will know that they see through all deception and lies.

They cannot be corrupted by the views of their parents or caretakers.

They cannot be corrupted by the old guard.

They speak-out against injustice and fraud.

They feel the pain of their Earth Mother and nature as the old guard pollutes and destroys Her.

They understand the God-connection better than those who currently teach it.

Each one was born in the fourth dimension or higher and understands the power that love has over all.

Many are light bearers, psychics, empaths, natural healers, or telepathic from birth. Some were born into families of light who have guided these children to even more spiritual awareness.

Others were born into families entrapped by the old guard thinking and have suffered greatly from the superstitious beliefs of their families. They have been falsely diagnosed and medicated heavily in an effort to destroy the natural gifts of love to which they were born. But the gifts are not lost or destroyed. The Indigo children have claimed their gifts and what God has given to them, no man can ever take away.

The old guard crucifies, imprisons, or dismembers the prophets sent to free the masses. They have attempted to do the same with Indigo children but in this case there are too many to crucify, too many to imprison, too many to dismember for the Indigo children have come to Earth by the millions and they will be heard.

You, as adults of this time, would be wise to listen to the children who have been in your care.

They have much to teach you but more importantly they will help to free you.

The forerunner to the Indigoes entered this Earth plane as early as the 1950s. They trickled in to prepare the way. Many were considered rebels, those who disregarded society's mores when in reality they saw through the injustices of segregation and other such regulations that perpetuated separation rather than oneness.

Each year a few more were incarnated until finally in the year 2000 over two million were living on Earth's plane; sent to prepare you for a better way and to teach you how to manifest this new era

.

Question 11

How will the Indigo children help usher in this new era?

They will teach you a new way. They will usher in the new era. Even now they know the possibilities of what is to come. They see through the distortions and illusions of mankind.

The Indigo child cannot be deceived. They look at those who lie to them with clarity and see the lie clearly. Even if you have punished them for naming the lie, even if you have subdued them with authority, they see the lie.

Many may have conformed on the outside but on the inside they are true to their cause. The Indigo child has strength of character and cannot be broken. The fear in mankind tries to break this but love is stronger than fear.

The Indigo children are united in their cause. The Indigo forerunners have prepared the way for the children to execute their plan.

Question 12

What is the plan of the Indigo children?

The Indigo children bring peace and unity to the world. They will see the new age ushered in. Their vision is oneness and hope. They see the threads of light that connect the All to the All That Is.

They will use the gifts of love to unify the world.

They are not afraid.

They will teach fearlessness to you, the adults of this world.

Question 13

Is the message of the Indigo children also your true message?

My message is always love.

All prophets brought the message of love but fear rose up and destroyed the message of love.

The Indigo children also bring the message of love but there are too many to destroy. Fear will not destroy these children or their message.

The message of love will be heard.

The message of love will set you free

Question 14

Your intended message was love but over the centuries it has become distorted. Will you tell us the reality of your life's true message Vs the teaching and doctrines of today?

Doctrine: We believe in one God, the Father, the Almighty, maker of heaven and earth, of all that is, seen and unseen.

Truth: There is but one God, the Father, the Almighty, maker of heaven and earth, of all that is, seen and unseen.

Doctrine: We believe in one Lord, Jesus Christ, the only Son of God, eternally begotten of the Father, God from God, Light from Light, true God from true God, begotten, not made, of one

Being with the Father. Through him all things were made.

Truth: There is but one God and all are His/Her children. Jesus Christ was begotten of the woman, Mary, and a highly evolved being from another realm.

Doctrine: For us and for our salvation he came down from heaven: by the power of the Holy Spirit he became incarnate from the Virgin Mary, and was made man.

Truth: I was born of a woman and conceived as any other man/woman. I incarnated to show mankind that as sons and daughters of God all are equal and all might have the gifts of the Spirit as I did.

Doctrine: For our sake he was crucified under Pontius Pilate; he suffered death and was buried. On the third day he rose again in accordance with the Scriptures; he ascended into heaven and is seated at the right hand of the Father.

Truth: I was crucified, I suffered death and was buried. On the third day I rose in spiritual form to show my brothers and sisters that death is not the end; that life is eternal, and that as the sons and daughters of God we are equally beloved children.

Doctrine: He will come again in glory to judge the living and the dead, and his kingdom will have no end.

Truth: The Christ revealed himself in spiritual form to many after his resurrection. The spiritual form of all is pure light for they have returned to their Father/Mother, the Source of

Light. The kingdom of God has no end; it is eternal as the spiritual form is eternal.

Doctrine: We believe in the Holy Spirit, the Lord, the giver of life, who proceeds from the Father.

Truth: The spiritual form of Christ was perceived as pure light. Those who saw it could only name it "Holy". All spiritual forms emanate from the Source of all light, the Father, therefore all are holy.

Doctrine: With the Father and the Son he is worshiped and glorified. He has spoken through the Prophets.

Truth: God has always sent His/Her message through the prophets. Mankind has killed God's prophets. You are the sons and daughters of God, as are the prophets that were sent before and after. All are God's children.

Doctrine: We believe in one holy catholic and apostolic Church.

Truth: All paths lead to God. There is not one church or sect that has all the answers or truth for truth is eternal.

Doctrine: We acknowledge one baptism for the forgiveness of sins.

Truth: There are many paths to forgiveness of sins but all begin in the heart.

Doctrine: We look for the resurrection of the dead, and the life of the world to come. Amen

Truth: The dead are resurrected according to their beliefs. All beings of light return to the light. All of mankind are beings of light. It is the teachings of man that have confused the dead causing some to await the return of Christ, others to lie in their graves, and others to wander the earth. Those who easily return to the light understand this regardless of the false teaching received in this plane.

Question 15

Why is the discrepancy so great between your intentions and the doctrine that has survived?

My intentions were to unite all of mankind and this could only be accomplished with love and from the heart.

Unity is not usually beneficial to governmental or church sects and their leadership. Unity in essence is love without segregation or separation by race, creed, color, gender or sexual orientation.

In unity, mankind will not take from another country or individual what does not belong to them.

In unity, mankind will not kill in the name of God for God is the Father/Mother of all.

In unity, mankind does not warmonger other nations for their goods and resources only to benefit a few and starve the masses.

Unity does not usually benefit those in power. They use fear to control and hate for power. And so, those in power have always changed my teachings to suit their needs for power and control to further their personal interests.

Question 16

Not to be disrespectful, but how do we know the truth of what you are saying now?

You have always known the truth. Even as a small child sitting beside your parents on the pew you knew what sounded true and what did not. You looked to the face of your parents to see if they too knew the truth and even when you knew they did not, you still believed what your heart told you.

You questioned what you heard and asked questions that no one could answer. This confirmed what you already knew – these leaders spouted words that they did not believe or understand. How can they understand without faith, and how can they have faith without love?

You have always known the truth.

You know that you are more than a body that turns to dust.

You know that there is a God, a power that is greater than anything, that loves and cares for you.

You know that there is eternal life after death.

You know that God is love and that He/She does not punish others for their differences.

You know that God is God of All.

You know that you are not alone in this vast universe.

You know that God is in you and all around you.

You know that you have gifts and abilities that you hide from others out of fear.

You know that Angels have protected you.

You know that there are no coincidences.

You know that I speak the truth to you now.

You know that your news media has deceived you.

You know that your churches have deceived you.

You know that in general you have been lied to.

You know all of these things and much more because your heart knows the truth.

Question 17

All these things you have said as truth resonate with me as true but how do others who are reading this know they are true?

They can only know truth from the heart. Jump into the heart so that you may be free. Test these truths from the heart.

For those who have picked up this book without reading Books 1 & 2, stop now and place your right hand over the physical location of the heart. Feel the heartbeat in your chest. With each beat repeat "Thank you. Thank you." Be ever conscious of the heart and your gratitude. This is the first step to living in the heart. This is the place to begin.

Test the truth of each statement from the heart. The heart is your pure connection to God. It is in the heart that all truth is known.

Question 18

We have elected officials and those in high positions who don't teach us these things. Even in the churches this information is not taught. Why don't our leaders know these things?

For the most part, mankind is trapped in the third dimension of the ego – including worldwide leaders in all areas of government and religion. They do not teach you these things because they do not know. How can they when the ego does not see beyond itself? The ego is not consciously connected to the needs of others.

The ego does its work for selfish reasons. It is concerned with more, not better. Even if shown a method that is more environmentally sound the ego refuses to change.

Only when mankind moves into the fourth dimension, into the heart, will there be changes that reach beyond the self, beyond selfishness. These changes will embrace the world and all of its inhabitants as one in complete unity.

Right now there is plenty of food so that none would go hungry. Right now there is plenty of water so that none would thirst. Right now there is plenty of energy so that the entire world would stay warm and dry.

It is the selfishness of the ego and the old guard way of thinking that prevents this. It is the selfishness of the ego that hoards more than enough for a few and allows the rest of the world to do without.

The pattern is repeated through each generation and has become routine or standard practice in businesses, families and in the churches. Each one doing as their forefathers did before them, never questioning, never understanding and forever digging a rut that becomes a grave.

The only way to break free of these patterns is to crack open the heart, to live in the heart. The heart is where you find the truth and live the truth.

The heart will never deceive you or lead you astray. The heart will show you the way to truth and to true change.

Question 19

All that you have just said seems to be in opposition to what most religions leaders teach. How did the messages in the bible get turned upside down or wrong-side out?

What I have to say may be considered blasphemy, but it must be said -- man wrote the bible. Man received inspiration from God but the message was filtered through the ego's hunger for power and greed.

The Old Testament was written to control the Jewish race and to strike fear in the hearts of all who would oppose them. The New Testament was written to control the Gentiles and to strike fear in the hearts of those who did not follow its precepts.

God did not intend for you to live in fear. God is love. God did not intend for you to believe that only one group of people are His/Her children. You are all the children of God and you are equal in His/Her eyes.

It does not matter if you are the beggar on the street or the ruler in high places; you are all equal in His/Her eyes. Your spirit is Divine and therefore you are Divine. You have lived many lives, sometimes as the beggar, sometimes as the ruler. You have been crucified; you have been the one to crucify. You have been the slave and you have been the master. In this plane of third dimension, you have merely forgotten who you are.

Wake up to the power that is within you!

You are a child of God, a Divine multidimensional being of light. Awaken now to the power that you hold. Cast off the chains that have bound you.

Question 20

You mentioned that we have been protected by Angels. To my knowledge, I have never seen an Angel. How have we been protected?

Angels are all around you. They travel unseen doing the work of God but they can manifest in human form when necessary. All of you have experienced this even without your knowing or understanding.

Angels carry out the will of God. They protect and serve mankind in general according to the directive of God. They protect and serve mankind individually also according to the directive of God.

You are never alone.

Question 21

What is the difference between spirit guides and Angels?

Each individual is accompanied by at least one spiritual guide when they incarnate into this earthly plane. Some of you have one or two; others have a multitude of spiritual guides with you depending on how large the scope of your work is during this incarnation. You choose your spiritual companions before you incarnate. You choose from a pool of loved ones who have the strengths and characteristics you will rely on while in physical form.

You are never alone.

Angels on the other hand come to assist or protect you during critical times. They bring messages of comfort or hope. They move obstacles out of your way. They cover your body with a protective force field when necessary.

Angels are sent by God.

God, the Divine Mind, is ever aware of your circumstances and situations and knows when you are in need of outside help. Angels are sent to minister unto you, to assist you, to comfort you but never to interfere. They can appear in human form or in their full glory with angelic wings. Most often they appear in human form as a stranger who just happened to be in the right place during your time of need.

All have been visited by Angels.

Question 22

How do Angels minister unto us, assist or comfort us?

There are many ways:

When you are weak, they bring you strength.

When you are fearful, they bring you courage.

When you are ready to give up, they bring you hope.

When you are tired and hungry, they refresh you.

When you are in danger, they shield you.

Angels cannot change the course of your path or interfere in your life choices but they can assist you in completing your path and life choices. Angels assist you in finishing what you came here to accomplish.

Angels travel on this earthly plane doing the will of God. For the most part, they are unseen and unheard as they go about their work of ministering to God's Divine children.

Question 23

Why can't we see our spiritual guides and Angels?

Some do see into these unseen realms. Children see from birth until their parents teach them not to see. For the most part, mankind does not see because he/she does not believe.

It is not only the spiritual guides and Angels that you do not see. You do not see what is all around you. You do not see the energy pattern in all of life or the auras that emanate from each individual. Your soul sees, but you do not see with your natural eyes.

You have been blinded to these sights and wonders just as you are blind to the suffering of others.

Question 24

If children are born seeing into the unseen realm, why do they stop seeing?

A child is born more aware of spirit than body. In this awareness, the child sees all aspects of the spirit world. As the child grows, he/she must learn to manipulate the body and becomes more conscious of the physical than the spiritual world. When the child begins to talk, the parents train the child as they were trained by their parents and past generations. The parent scolds the child for any mention of what is unseen or unknown to the parent until finally the child stops seeing because he believes the parent over his own eyes.

This also happens with adults. The group mind of the third dimension is the parent. Anyone who sees outside the group mind is scolded or punished until they stop seeing and believe the parent/group mind over their own eyes.

Question 25

What does the group mind not want us to see?

You have been given many messages from cave wall drawings to ancient manuscripts. You have looked into the sky and seen strange things that cannot be explained by your governmental officials. You allow those in power to hide the truth from you. You allow your past history to become myths and metaphorical stories. All these things and more represent the struggle between the third dimension/current group mind and the fourth dimension/future group mind.

Question 26

What are we missing; why are we blind?

You want me to tell you exactly what has been hidden from you but that is not the purpose of this dialogue. You must awaken to the truth for yourselves.

Acknowledge that you have been lied to. Seek the truth. Live from the heart which knows only truth. Pray that more will awaken in the heart. Demand change so that your chains may be broken and cast off. Know that you are children of an All Powerful God and receive your inheritance of Divinity.

As divine children you cannot be enslaved without allowing enslavement. You cannot be lied to without allowing the lies. You allow what is happening to you by your very actions or inaction in many cases. Your free-will controls your fate. Use this divine gift to change everything.

I say again, use your free-will to change everything.

You have the power to stop the enslavement. You have the power to change the old guard. You have the power to usher in this new era of fourth dimension. You must simply embrace the Divine gift of free-will.

Question 27

Please explain more about free-will and how we use it or embrace it?

Each individual is born with the Divine gift of free-will. You begin to give this power away as children when your parents first scold you for seeing what they cannot see. This prepares you to hand over more of your gift in school and later in the work place until finally you become just like everyone else – blind to all the spiritual forces around you. It is a process and has been aptly called "domestication" of the human race.

Anyone who refuses to give over their power is ridiculed or punished by the third dimension group mind. You are outcast. You do not follow the rules. Some are even diagnosed and medicated in an effort to force them to conform; others are exiled or locked away from society.

To embrace your free-will you must take back your power. You must jump into the heart and live in truth. Follow the process of living in the heart as described earlier in these books.

This is the first step to taking back your personal and spiritual power. When you live in the heart, you live in truth. When you live in truth, you understand your free-will and use it appropriately and automatically.

Question 28

What changes do we need to make to move into the fourth dimension and use our free-will most effectively?

Let me say again, so that you understand fully. Use free-will to jump into the heart. Use free will to remove the old guard from power and replace it with love.

The process is this:

You must first use free-will to choose the heart over the ego for yourselves and your family. This is jumping into the heart, a leap of faith. This is a choice you make by exercising your free-will.

Free-will declares: I will be free!

Then you work with the heart and from the heart in gratitude to understand love of all things, the oneness of all things and that you are the Divine children of God.

Next, you open to the truth of the heart. You test all things from the heart so that you cannot be deceived or enslaved.

And lastly, from the heart you manifest the desires of the heart to your highest good and to the highest good of all concerned.

This is the way you move from third dimension to fourth dimension. This is the way that the fourth dimension and free-will work together for the good of all.

Question 29

How will we know when we have moved from the third dimension to the fourth dimension… what changes will we notice?

In the third dimension the ego rules. The ego is concerned only with power and control. It is never concerned with the welfare of others, only with self. Sometimes this "self" refers to a group such as governmental leaders or church officials. Other times it relates only to the individual self – the desires that anyone might have for self-preservation.

In the third dimension future consequences are ignored. Whether this relates to the individual family unit or countries, the result is the same. The predominant thought is "more".

In the family, the father and mother work long hours and strive to attain more while their children are left without guidance. In the governments of the world, leaders arm their borders to protect their starving citizens. In each case, the parents and the governments are blind to the consequences of actions they have created from the ego.

Currently, individuals are forced to work in jobs where they have little aptitude for that particular job. They only work for the pay. There is little joy or satisfaction from the work itself. This rapes the soul of mankind. It is one of the deepest violations of the human spirit.

When the group mind moves to the fourth dimension, all decisions will be made from the heart. Fathers and mothers will put the welfare of their children first. Corporations will honor this decision and other parents and corporations will see the wisdom in these choices. World governments will put the welfare of their citizens first. They will provide food, shelter and clothing for all. These governments will set the example for others to follow.

Individuals will be encouraged to pursue their dreams and the jobs for which they are best suited. The arts and teaching professions will be honored and seen for what they are – opportunities to feed the soul of mankind.

Those who use their gifts of spirit will no longer be seen as eccentric or insane, they will be honored as leaders of the people and healers of the world.

The changes that you will notice when the group mind has changed to fourth dimension are vast. This is a time of awakening for all who choose it.

Question 30

Will all move into the fourth dimension at the same time?

Moving into the fourth dimension is a choice; it is utilizing the gift of free-will. Not all will make this choice and of those who do, not all will make this choice at the same time.

There are always forerunners and currently there are many today who have already made the choice to move into the fourth dimension. When enough of you have chosen this, the group mind will shift accordingly.

Not all are in the same dimension at any given time. Even in the group mind today, there are those who live in the fourth through the seventh dimensions. As always it is your individual choice and free-will to change yourself and evolve. With that choice the numbers grow as you set the example until finally the group mind changes.

Question 31

How many of us must make the choice to live in the fourth dimension before the group mind changes?

The choice is made individually and the change occurs individually. As each one makes the decision, he/she moves into the heart dimension immediately. When others see the changes in you it allows them to also make the conscious decision to live in the heart. It is a ripple effect.

I suspect that your question is about the specific number that is required before the shift from third to fourth dimension occurs in mankind. To that I will say that when the group mind is overrun by fourth dimension thought patterns, then the change will occur globally and mankind will no longer be considered a third dimension world.

Let me be clear; not all will choose to live in fourth dimension just as currently not all live in third dimension. The shift into fourth dimension is a necessary part of your human development.

Question 32

What will cause others to make the decision to change?

In order for others to want to change, they must first see the benefit of the change around them and in others. Change is facilitated by being exposed to the light; to truth.

The light bearer brings light to dark places.

The inspired word opens the heart to truth.

The Indigo children point the way to freedom.

Allow the light bearer's light to shine on you without fear. Do not run from the light. Examine yourself in the light and make the necessary changes.

When you read any of the many books written about spiritual laws, transformation and enlightenment, allow your heart to open to the messages. Let the seeds of possibility be planted so that they might grow into wisdom. Do not shun new information simply because you have not heard it before. Test what you are reading and hearing from the heart and allow it to take root in you.

The Indigo children lead the way. Let the children be your guides to freedom. They have not yet been corrupted by handed-down tradition. They remain pure in their understanding of how the world works. Allow them to remain free and to lead you into liberty.

Question 33

How do we know which material and books are truly inspired?

You are right to ask this question. There has been much about the inspired word of God. And God does inspire all written words regardless of their context and subject matter.

The true question is how to know if the material and books are purely inspired. God inspires and man/woman filters this inspiration through their experiences. Most of the time the end results is not what was originally intended. The bible is a good example of how God's inspiration has been filtered from its original intent. It would be accurate to say that it was truly inspired but inaccurate to say that it was purely inspired.

Even channeling is filtered by the individual or vessel that channels the spirit causing the content to be lost or changed unless the man/woman tests for truth from the heart for exact wording.

You will know which material and books are inspired from its effect on the heart. Let me caution you that not all books and material that overwhelm you with fear are evil or negative. The ego is often threatened by change and new material. It rears an ugly head when the old guard thinking is challenged.

You must always test from the heart to know the truth of the matter.

Question 34

How do we test from the heart if we are still in the third dimension and caught in the old guard thinking pattern?

If you have chosen to move into the fourth dimension and live in the heart, you are not caught in the old guard thinking pattern. You can successfully test from the heart. There will be many times that the ego will try to take back your power and control you but that does not mean it can pull you back into the third dimension. Your free-will has chosen to live in the heart.

Free-will is your most amazing Divine right.

Free-will sets your desires in motion by the simple act of choice.

Free-will moves heaven and earth.

Question 35

If the ego battles for control even after we have moved into the heart dimension, can it take back our power and free-will causing us to return to the third dimension?

The ego can rear its ugly head and attempt to take back your power but it cannot take your free-will. Free-will has always belonged to mankind exclusively. You can give up free-will but it cannot be taken from you.

Any individual can move into a different dimension by choosing to do so. It is a conscious choice of free-will. Since free-will is the factor, it is possible for the individual to choose to live in the ego dimension again.

I ask you – will you choose to move into the ego after having lived in the heart? It is unlikely that any would make this choice.

Question 36

Although it is unlikely, what would cause an individual to return to the ego after living in the heart?

Humans are multidimensional beings – body, mind and soul – but dual in nature – flesh and spirit or human and divine.

Human nature holds onto old grievances; feels the pain of loss and the sorrow of guilt. Human nature blames others and refuses to see God at work in all situations. Human nature relies on self for reconciliation and vengeance.

The divine nature is to forgive; to love without reason and let go knowing that God is in charge. The divine nature sees the oneness in all and the divine nature of all. The divine nature understands that everything has its purpose, even pain and sorrow, in the bigger picture of the Universe.

When an individual returns to the ego, it is usually because he/she cannot let go and let God. It is usually because he is consumed by the idea that he must make a situation or person "right" by his own power and control. She wallows in the pain, sorrow and blame until she turns away from the heart.

Question 37

People turn away from God also. What causes this to happen?

Some who turn away from God are heartbroken.

They have been taught a set of principles and beliefs by either church or family that are not understood by either the teacher or the student. In their time of need, when they or a loved one is in danger, they call out to these principles and beliefs asking to be saved from the danger. When their salvation does not come, they are downcast and heartbroken.

It is not because God did not answer, it is because the principles and beliefs are faulty. The principles and beliefs themselves are broken, not God.

Question 38

Are you saying that we have to know the "correct" principles and beliefs in order for God to answer our prayers?

I say that these individuals have more faith in the principles or rules than they have in God.

I say that these individuals put their faith in rules without understanding or wisdom.

I say that the individual suffers from false teachings, whether family, church or government, teaches them.

I say that when you come to God with understanding and wisdom, He/She hears your prayers.

Question 39

You mentioned that crossing-over departed spirits is one of our many gifts. Why is it necessary to cross-over departed spirits?

Being dual in nature – human and divine – is often confusing to the individual while incarnated. Is it any wonder that a recently departed spirit would be confused as well?

When an individual body dies, the spirit lives on but the memories of the current life are predominantly in focus for the spirit. The teachings they accepted are part of those memories.

Society rarely teaches the individual how to live. It is even more unusual that society teaches you how to die. Departed spirits are often confused and wander about looking for answers, staying near loved ones and even remembering their death incessantly.

Helping these confused and lost spirits return to the light is a unique gift. It is a gift that anyone can have but few choose it as the gift they are willing to own.

Question 40

There are popular television shows that talk about ghosts, mediums, etc. Is crossing-over departed spirits anything like what we see on television?

Only a very few of those who cross-over departed spirits help the dead solve their problems or unfinished business; those who do have been accurately depicted on television for the most part.

It is much more common for the person who crosses-over departed spirits to feel the presence of the spirit but recognizes that it is different than the presence of Angels or spiritual companions and guides.

The person who crosses-over departed spirits is sensitive to the spirit realm.

They may not hear the spirit speak but they sense that the spirit needs help; they sense why the spirit is there.

The person who crosses-over departed spirits has the ability to "bring down" white light and open a doorway in the white light to the other side.

The person who crosses-over departed spirits gives simple instructions to the spirit about crossing over.

The person who crosses-over departed spirits says prayers for the departed souls if this is requested.

The person who crosses-over departed spirits feels intense satisfaction after helping the spirits return to the light.

Question 41

Many of the gifts you mentioned have been the cause of people being burned at the stake or locked away in institutions in the not so distant past. What makes it different to own these gifts now?

In the past the world was filled with superstitious and dark beliefs generated by those in power. It was a means to control the masses. The leaders of that time did not wish for peasants to procure the same enlightened message they sought from their own prophets and seers.

It is similar to the new ruler who beheads all the male children in a conquered city. He does not desire to be challenged in the future; therefore, he annihilates all threats from the beginning.

The rulers of the past, both political and religious, were the same. Anyone who had a gift was seen as a threat. Sometimes anyone who knew of others who possessed these gifts was also a threat. It was a very dark time.

Today, it is more acceptable to have these gifts. During and after the shift the world will look to those who possess these gifts with respect and honor.

Question 42

There are many today that are called "sensitives" because they are sensitive to what others cannot see or hear. It is common for these individuals to be heavily medicated and labeled as mentally ill. Is it possible that this is another form of power and control; another way to stop enlightenment?

Many of those labeled mentally ill are created by the very system of the current world, the old guard thinking.

An individual who continues to see into the spiritual realm after a certain age of childhood is shunned and criticized. For many, this is enough to blind their sight. For others, they accept their sight but also accept the labels of insane or crazy that is often attached to them.

Even now there are prophets and seers locked away because they hear voices or see what others cannot. There are visionaries institutionalized because they have visions and dream dreams. There are mediums heavily medicated so that their gift is drowned in a sea of stupor.

There are very few educational tools available to these individuals. There is little training to assist in using these gifts to the highest good of all concerned. Those who are lucky enough to find a small group of similar souls close themselves off in seclusion.

This will change during and after the great shift that is on the horizon. And so, to those who are cloistered in seclusion I say, be brave, be bold and assist others to manage their budding gifts now. Do not hide but come out of hiding and teach others what you have already learned.

Question 43

Are there really Aliens who visit Earth in UFO's?

You ask this when you already know the answer. Do you ask for yourself or for the others reading this material? They also know the answer. The answer is inside each of you. And, as if that is not enough, the written and recorded proof has been with you throughout the ages.

Look to the heart to verify this.

Your governments work in close association with these beings and have for generations. The Universe has sent messages through writers and producers during the last century. Archeologist and scientist have hard evidence of historical events. Your military has covered up more evidence. It is all there for you to see but you do not open your eyes. You remain blind by choice.

Question 44

Why such a big cover-up?

The old guard desires to keep this information hidden for their own purposes of power and control. It is the same, ago-old story. By hiding the truth from the masses, they feel elitist. They are privy to a form of enlightenment that makes them superior to those who are unaware.

The old guard foolishly believes that mankind is incapable of accepting the truth about the Universe.

The old guard foolishly believes that he/she is superior to mankind in general.

The old guard foolishly believes that mankind will panic and destroy itself if the truth of other life is known.

The old guard foolishly underestimates mankind.

Question 45

How does the truth get revealed? How do we show others the information that has been hidden by the old guard?

Never in the history of mankind has there been so much information readily available to each individual. It is at your very fingertips. It is there for you to find.

Research. Find the answers that are available to you and test them from the heart. Know what you believe. Know that the beliefs you own are yours and not what has been passed down to you. Know that the beliefs you own are truth.

Always test the truth of your beliefs from the heart.

Live from the heart and it will lead you to all truth. The heart does not fear or quake in the light of new information. It is open to understanding and wisdom. Trust the heart to lead you to the answers you seek.

Question 46

Why would our world governments make an alliance with Aliens in the first place? What do they hope to gain?

For the most part, Aliens are higher evolved beings. You refer to them as alien because they are unfamiliar to you and because they are from a different place. As higher evolved beings that are capable of time and space travel; it is reasonable that they have technology and knowledge that is desirable to world leaders.

World leaders and governments, even religious leaders, are covetous of this technology. When these leaders do not see themselves equal to mankind in general, when they see mankind as slaves or as merely the uneducated masses they put their own welfare above yours. They look only to their own personal gain and power. In short, they sell out mankind to further their own interests.

Question 47

From what you have said and from other information I have studied it is obvious that our world leaders are not looking out for our best interest. How do we protect ourselves?

You have been given the tools and with the great shift that is on the horizon you will free yourselves from bondage. When you come from a place in the heart, from truth, no man can stand against you.

It is imperative to act now; to prepare yourselves. To live from the heart as all these messages have directed. It is your salvation. It is your freedom. It is your choice.

Question 48

You said that no man can stand against us, but what about the Aliens with advanced technology?

My brothers and sisters, do you not understand your Divinity? Do you not understand your free-will?

Higher evolved beings must respect your directive of free-will. All beings must respect mankind's divine gift and inheritance.

These beings work with your leaders because you have given over your power to these leaders. You look to them for all answers and all decisions never exercising your own divine right. You allow them to govern you, to pass laws for their personal benefit, to tax your wages for their personal vendettas. You tithe to the religious leaders never questioning their use of these monies. You do not hold your leaders accountable. You do not demand a reckoning. You simply go about your lives trusting what should not be trusted, following the path the old guard has set for you.

I say again, it is imperative that you awaken now! Let the scales fall from your eyes. Take back your power. Do not fear the old guard. It is only by joining in one voice that the old guard will fall to its knees and the new era will unfold. It begins with you. It begins with exercising your free-will!

Demand to see change!

Question 49

I have read that there are several types of Aliens that come to our world. Some are looking out for our best interest; some are impartial and merely watch, while others are only interested in our resources. Is any of this true?

All of this is true. Earth and humankind is one of the most beloved planetary systems in the Universes. Many have watched and studied your evolution. Many have taken advantage of the plentiful resources available. Many have intervened on your behalf as you have struggled for enlightenment and freedom from oppression. Others on occasion have saved you from self-destruction.

Now more than ever, the planetary visitations continue. You have but to open your eyes to see this.

Question 50

If we truly desire to be awakened to these events, how do we open our eyes to them?

First you must desire to awaken, to see what is going on right over your heads and all around you.

Then you must trust the heart that you will see the truth and only the truth.

You must exercise your divine right of free-will by choosing to see the truth that the heart will show you.

Finally, you accept the truth for what it is never recoiling when it appears to you but rather to nod your head in agreement as if to say, "Ahh, this is what I have been missing."

It sounds simple, almost too simple, but it is the way of opening the eyes to truth. It is a process that takes practice just as living in the heart takes practice. You must practice this daily if you desire to remove the scales from your eyes that have been put there by the old guard, by past beliefs and patterns.

The scales that cover your eyes are layers that must be peeled away but this is where you begin until finally you see clearly what has been hidden from you and those around you.

Question 51

I can imagine finally seeing what has been hidden from me, looking up and seeing the evidence of interplanetary visitations. But what if others do not practice these steps to open their eyes... What happens when I am the only one in the vicinity seeing these things?

Do not be afraid.

You envision the witch hunts of the past -- that once your eyes have been opened you will be singled out for punishment.

This is not the case in this new era. As you open your eyes so will others until finally those who cannot see will be the minority.

There is a tipping-point where when the threshold is reached, the consciousness of the group mind shifts into the new understanding.

Do not be afraid but rather desire to be a forerunner in this awakening.

Question 52

What about Alien abductions and the terrible things that have been done to the abductees?

It is true that there have been those of mankind who have been abducted and studied in less than humane ways. It is true that because of your current beliefs these incidents are so foreign to you that the logical mind easily dismisses these events as a bad dream.

Test these things from the heart so that you may know the truth of the matter.

Always test everything from the heart. If someone says they have a message from God, test the truth of the message as well as the individual from the heart. If someone says they have a message from The Christ, again test from the heart. If someone has a message from an Alien race, test from the heart.

It is the truth that sets you free!

Question 53

Are you concerned these words about Alien abduction will cause panic and fear in mankind?

That is the logic that the old guard has used to keep mankind in the dark about interplanetary visitations. It comes from fear not from heart-love.

The one key point of Alien abduction is that all beings must respect mankind's Divine directive of free-will. When free-will is exercised it must be honored. If an individual has been repeatedly abducted by an Alien race, that individual has not yet exercised his free-will. He has not stated, "I choose no more!"

If the individual keeps quiet about the abduction and allows the behavior to continue then he has not exercised his free-will. Free-will is choosing. The individual chooses that the abductions stop and they do.

Only through exercising your free-will do you begin to take back your personal power, that power you have allowed the old guard to own.

There is no need to be afraid of Aliens. They must honor your free-will.

Question 54

You have said that we must test the truth from the heart and exercise our free-will but fear has been deeply implanted in mankind in every movie about Aliens and by our governments' deeply secretive actions. How can we test from the heart when we are afraid?

    The old guard would have you ignorant and terrified, as slaves who have no understanding or knowledge of the workings of governments and leaders. They do not see you as individuals but rather as a herd of sheep that must be led to and from. They see the world's population much like a pyramid with you at the bottom while they are at the top. They do not appreciate that the bottom is the base that upholds the top. You have allowed this way of thinking to continue since time began.

As those who have allowed it, you are responsible for stopping it now. It cannot be done by fear or warfare. It can only be done by choice – free-will from the heart.

First, be conscious of the physical location of the heart. Notice its place inside the body, listen to the heartbeat. Become one with the heart.

Then, allow your individual selves to issue forth thanksgiving and gratitude with each heartbeat. Let it flow throughout the body daily. This is living in the heart.

Next, learn to test for truth but always test directly from the heart by involving the heart. Place your hand over the heart to remind yourself where to find the truth.

Only love and its derivatives are found in the heart – love, joy, peace, oneness, trust, faith, compassion, empathy and all the positive aspects of love.

Only fear and its derivatives are found in the ego – fear, hate, separation, revenge, selfishness and all the negative aspects of fear.

Question 55

From your previous answers, it sounds as if a great deal of information has been hidden from mankind. I am still not certain how we as a body of individuals can change the old guard. We have been separated from each other by our beliefs. Even new age believers are separated from other sects and groups. What are we to do to unite?

It is true that your beliefs have separated you from others. It is also true that when you live in the heart that the oneness of all emerges and becomes vividly alive.

It might be considered ironic that new age beliefs are not new at all. This is the proof that Universe has been sending messages as well as signs and symbols to mankind all along. These beliefs are pointing the way, as all messengers of God have always done. The difference at this time is that there are many messengers. They come to you with truth and possibilities of a better way.

It is the new age group as a whole that has opened to their spiritual gifts while Christianity and other sects have rebuked these same gifts. It is the new age group as a whole that has recognized there is more available in the spiritual world than the same old dead churches with the same cold messages. It is the new age group as a whole that has continued to seek while Christianity and other sects have convinced themselves that they have enough.

So I ask you, which group is following the leading of Spirit? Which group is growing in Spirit and spiritual awareness? Is it those who refuse to budge or is it those who desire more of God's kingdom?

To join or unite, all believers must see the oneness and Divinity of each other, each individual. Oneness is from the heart. Separation is from the ego.

Put aside your concepts of right and wrong. Put aside your divisions of doctrine and creed. Put aside your elitist attitudes that only a few are deserving. Put aside the beliefs that have been handed down to you for generations, the beliefs of the old guard. These are not your beliefs. They are the beliefs you have adopted from others.

Open to the heart and allow the truth to set you free from these old chains and restrictions. It is in the heart that you will find the truth of God's message. It is in the heart that you will be free from something that was never yours to begin with.

If you will die for your beliefs, if you will go to war for your doctrines, will these beliefs be your own or those of someone else?

The call for unity is set forth now. Unite in love and oneness for it is the only way to cut the divisions from your belief.

Question 56

Is it truly possible for the world to unite in this way?

It is. The world is ready for this change. Mankind is ready for this change. Many now pray for change.

It is the individual who will make the change first before the group can unite. By living in the heart the change will happen. For some the change will be immediate, for others it will be a gradual change, and still for others they will practice for some time to allow the heart to lead them. Any difficulty is due to old beliefs that are deeply ingrained in them but with desire for change, change will occur.

You create your reality, each and every one of you.

For the reality to change, your dream or desire must change first. The desire for unity will then become the group dream.

You create your reality by the desires of your heart.

The Universe/God manifests those dreams.

Your task is then to get out of the way and to allow God to manifest the desires of your heart.

Question 57

It sounds so simple and yet I have personally had difficulty manifesting my dreams. What am I doing wrong?

There is no right or wrong, only what is and what creative force you apply to desires. Each step you take gets you closer to effectively creating the desires of the heart.

Most of you who are working with manifesting your dreams insist that you must manifest or bring into reality by your intention alone. Manifesting for the individual is to make real. Let me be clear.

The Universe/God manifests.

You dream.

Here are the steps: You dream the desire or you desire the dream. Either way, you create the dream in your thoughts. You visualize yourself within the dream which makes it real to you. You reconcile that only God manifests the dream in your life – God brings it into existence. You get out of the way and allow God to do His/Her work. Finally, the only thing left for you to do is hold tight to the dream. Don't give up or change the dream to another dream while the manifesting process takes place. Allow God to manifest your dream. Give thanks when it is done.

Question 58

Do we each have a specific Life-Path that we have come to accomplish?

Each individual chose a path or challenge for this incarnation. You selected the basic ingredients for this lifetime that were conducive to accomplishing this goal. You selected spiritual companions to accompany you on this journey; those who you felt would benefit you and remind you of your destination. You selected individual family and friends who would challenge you and the individual experiences that would shape your life. You selected individuals who would briefly come into your life during times of need; those who had a message to inspire you or assist you in attaining your goal.

Then, as with all souls who incarnate, you passed through the birth canal from one dimension to another, leaving spiritual understanding behind and taking on the task of physical understanding.

From birth to age two you floated between the worlds as you accepted the challenges of mastering the physical body. Your path has always been to find your way home to the Source from whence you came. The specific challenge you chose lays the course for that journey.

Question 59

Does this earthly journey include our quest for spiritual wisdom?

There are many paths that the individual soul can choose, but all paths involve understanding and spiritual growth or wisdom.

Love	Hate
Courage	Fear
Wisdom	Ignorance
Forgiveness	Unforgiving
Abuse	Abuser

These are only a few of the paths but to fully understand love one must also understand hate. To understand courage, one must also understand fear, and so forth.

To attain spiritual wisdom, the soul experiences all aspects of each path.

Question 60

When a soul has chosen to understand love in all its fullness which includes understanding hate, can the soul get lost in the emotion of hate and therefore forget everything he/she came here to learn?

The individual always forgets why he is here but the soul remembers and learns from each experience. The individual is encased in the physical body and is limited by the material aspects of that burden. Only by tapping into the soul memories can the bigger picture be seen.

The hidden question you desire to ask is whether or not a soul can become so discouraged that they give up on the quest for understanding.

And I say that the soul does not give up but the individual sometimes does.

The individual will sometimes cry that life is too hard, that the journey is too difficult. The individual will sometimes refuse assistance from those she has chosen to give aid during this incarnation. The dream becomes too real. In such an example the individual does give up on the incarnation and the soul returns to the Source with those life memories to be refreshed and bathed in the Light of God/Universe.

Question 61

Is it possible for the soul to understand all the aspects of love in one incarnation?

There are many aspects of love:

Like

Infatuation

Platonic love

Filial love

Sibling love

Lust

Agape

Dislike

Hate

Abhorrence

These are only a few of the aspects of love. You can understand that it might take many incarnations to fully grasp all the aspects of love.

Question 62

On average, how many times does a soul incarnate before he/she is done?

Ha-Ha-Ha-Ha-Ha! My dear one, a soul is never done for when the soul has experienced the *all that there is* it begins again with the understanding that there is no beginning or end.

Life, as you think of it in this time and space, is circular. Where is the beginning or the end of a circle once it is drawn?

But to answer your question, a soul incarnates on average 500 times; some more, some less.

Sometimes the experiences that a soul desires to understand take him to distant planets. Other times the experiences desired exist in other realms.

Sometimes the soul desires to experience life as male; other times as female. And back and forth it goes…

Question 63

Is it discouraging to the soul to know that there is no end?

No, my sister, it is not discouraging to the soul.

If the individual life and body repeated the cycle without end, that would be discouraging. The soul is eternal. The body wears out and dies. The soul lives forever.

After each incarnation the soul returns to the Source of All. It is refreshed and learns from each incarnated life's memories. The soul can never die because the Source can never die. The soul is the essence of the Source. The Source is eternal therefore the soul is eternal.

Question 64

What about evolution and the big bang theory?

Scientists are a necessary part of planet Earth's history. The only problem is that scientists in general seek to prove concepts and theories without evidence of faith; they distance themselves from all that is metaphysical.

There are many metaphysical concepts that cannot be proven in the laboratory or by scientific measurements such as love, faith, hope and many others. The fact that these emotions cannot be measured in a test tube does not invalidate their reality. Many occurrences are beyond physical explanation.

Did human beings evolve from apes? No.

Was the Universe formed from the big bang theory? No

Will I give you proof? No.

There are many in the metaphysical community who understand the big bang theory in an enlightened manner. To them, God/Universe divided the Light Source into many sparks. Each spark of the Light Source resides inside each soul and each soul is in each individual thereby connecting all to the Source forevermore.

The metaphysical community also has an understanding of evolution that others would be wise to grasp. Each individual evolves spiritually as she transcends dimensions.

Question 65

I have received requests from readers who would like to know if you will answer questions they ask. Is this a possibility for another book?

I proposed that we write three books of 66 questions each for the original series when we started this session. This is nearing completion now.

It is understandable that this vessel has asked questions that were significant to her. It is also understandable how others reading these messages also have questions.

I will continue to answer questions through this vessel from others for a time.

Question 66

What are the guidelines for the questions?

The vessel will provide contact information for those who have additional questions.

The questions will not be repetitive of topics already covered in this series.

The questions will not be of a personal nature but rather of significance to all.

The questions will be carefully worded and succinct.

The request will be one question rather than a series of questions.

Through this vessel I will select the questions to be answered.

Until next time…

From the Author

If you enjoyed this book, please leave a review on Amazon, B&N, and Goodreads so that others can find this work.

If you have questions that you would pose to The Christ, send them by email to the following address:

AskingsCC@gmail.com

Thank you for your interest in this series of books.

CC Askings

Made in the USA
Charleston, SC
11 December 2015